A͏rs
P͏oetica

ArsPoetica is an imprint of Pisgah Press, LLC, established
in 2011 to publish and promote works of quality offering
original ideas and insight into the human condition, the
realm of knowledge, and the world around us.

Published by Pisgah Press, LLC
PO Box 9663, Asheville, NC 28815
www.pisgahpress.com

Cover illustration: "The Shaman," by Ayal Hurst
Photographs courtesy of Hawk Hurst

ISBN-978-1-942016-97-7
Poetry
First Printing
March 2025

Acknowledgements

To my husband Hawk, the one I waited for, who taught me about loving, and without whom none of my visions would have ever come to be; to Amanda, who dances in delight with me, and sees into the depths; to Mikki, who is always there weaving in the world with profound wisdom; and to Marilyn, who has known me longest of all, and who has never abandoned me. Thank you for your love and support. It has encouraged me to grow and to share that which is good and true.

WILD LIFE

Poems by
Ayal Hurst

ArsPoetica, an imprint of
Pisgah Press, LLC
PO Box 9663
Asheville, NC 28815
www.pisgahpress.com

Foreword

This life has been a search for finding what feels, to me, like the Ultimate Truth. If you had told me when I was growing up what I was going to do, or be, I probably would have said something like a lawyer or a doctor, as that is what my parents fervently hoped I would be. I never would have thought that my life would take the path it has, though now, knowing myself much better, I see that it was inevitable and definitely meant to be. It has led to wonderful adventures and amazing, mystical experiences. I have discovered many wondrous and magical things as I have walked this path.

To find this "Truth," I became well versed in many forms of alternative healing techniques and modalities, lived for a while in a yoga ashram, studying the ancient wisdom of the sages and the Vedas, spent time in sweat lodges and women's circles. Throughout it all, I studied with many wonderful spiritual teachers along the way. What I found was that Love, the unconditional kind, was always the answer, no matter what form my studies took. To be able to live from that level of Love, and/or to be able to share it, meant, I also found, that I had to let go of my own shadows and wounds and anything else that seemed to be in the way. It has been a lifelong, ongoing journey of discovery.

Writing and sharing these poems has been one of the ways for me to process and to share this journey, to voice it when it so strongly called out to be voiced, trying to put it into words when it was needing to be birthed and emerge into the light of day.

I hope that in them you will find something true that also resonates with your own, beautiful, ongoing journey and the spirit of your soul.

With blessings,

Ayal Hurst

Contents

Contents

Wild Life

Evolution

WILD LIFE

Poems by
Ayal Hurst

COSMIC DANCE

Ayal Hurst

The Soul of Eternity

The Soul of Eternity,
the web of Being and Non-being.
Never ending . . . the Alpha and Omega.
The Great Wheel, an infinite Spiral, spinning.
It throbs behind the yellow curtain, hidden,
the veil that shrouds the Sacred Eye.

Every star, each potential birth,
Fire, Love, and Magic,
immense Clouds of Music
meandering through the Universe.
Sacred veins pumping drops of liquid manna
through the leaves of trees,
through my skin, and in my blood,
through every cell.
This is the manifestation of Infinite Thought.
A sizzling serenity.
A soothing dream.
A fevered dream.
This is what comes
from voicing The Word.

Finding the Balance. Finding the Opening.
This is the trail I seek.
Wanting it more than life, to cross the Portal,
the reaches of a higher realm.
A fierce concentration must part that veil.
A level of consciousness beyond my ken.
I have only been there, once or twice.
Do I fear it? Perhaps.
Perhaps I only need to let it in.

Ayal Hurst

The Silver Sheath

The heart, a very resilient organ.
It forgives after being broken,
like a shell tossed ashore,
lying fractured from the storm,
with browning seaweed
and the cold remains of crabs.

The Heart births first.
It forms the body,
sending codes, unfathomable messages
to create the mystical potential for life.
All organs, tissues, muscles,
all cells and their functions
form from Her precise instructions.
She is a sacred microcosm of a vaster Heart,
born from the ceaseless love of Source.
As above, so below.

What she is, we take for granted.
That she will give life,
beat the rhythm of the Universe within our chest,
never ceasing.
She is beyond our understanding.
We think we have a name for her.
But she is Unknowable,
like the name of God.

A cave of crystal splendor,
she is protected by a Silver Sheath.
Only Love lives there.

Past, present, future, all are there.
She smiles, breathing Life into our bones.
The Galaxy lives within her,
ceiling and walls blazing
with stars nestled in the night sky.

She is the Great Mother, waiting to be known.
Living there, all hope will be ignited . . .
all things are possible. All dreams fulfilled.
The Universe unfolds, and you Remember.

Yet, without that Silver Sheath,
she is vulnerable, fine spun,
terrible in fragility.

The mightiest of all creations,
the Heart,
and yet, we must embrace it
as we would our first born child,
creating the most fierce boundaries,
loving beyond measure.
Entrusting it only
to those who carefully caress it,
holding it safely in a blanket of empathy
and the softest hands of kindness.

Ayal Hurst

Starlight

To claim the vision of my Life,
I must first accept
the perfection of it all.
If I accept the perfection of my life,
I accept my destiny.

I would say this:
that I am born of Starlight,
ethereal as the music of the spheres,
gliding on strands of incandescent flame
to reach the Earth below.

I do not claim the sun,
a fiercer source of light
that warms the essence of the world.
I do not claim
the cooler light of Mother Moon,
though she flows with silver brilliance,
and can teach me many things . . .
to let go, to shift my form,
to ride the waves of ebb and flow,
to lessen and complete.

I claim the Stars,
for their soft light
fills the velvet darkness.
Ithildin, it is called in Elvish.
Magic abides there,
the twinkling of fairy bells.
A beacon of what seems far away,
and yet never will abandon.

Night after night, they are there,
gazing down,
calling us to return,
to be more than we are,
to fly free
through the vastness of the Sky.

They are the Great Star Nation,
the campfires of the Ancestors.
Spirit canoes flowing
on the rivers of constellations,
from tribe to tribe,
from one star to another,
exchanging news and gifts of Light.
Neither hot, nor cold,
Starlight beckons.

In that protection,
knowing what I am,
I abide in safety.
Accepting my vision, unafraid.

Breakfast with Lao Tzu

I breakfast each morning with Lao Tzu.
He is a wonderful companion.
Eyes twinkling
through each hexagram
of the I Ching,
each paragraph of the Tao.

He Guides my way,
speaking to me across the Ages.
Across the vast mountains
of China
and deep seas,
through generations past,
and the darkened reaches
of Space and Time.

His Wisdom flows
into my cells,
as rain drops
fill a thirsty bud.

I call upon his words,
recounting them by heart.
The puzzle of being
made so explicitly clear.

Lullaby

Listen . . .
Soon the sun will set,
and Darkness will flow over a horizon
tinted with blue and gold,
veiling everything in an inky blanket
of softest velvet,
inset with crystal stars.

All the unresolved and hurtful things
that touched you
during the clarity of brilliant day
can be gently put to rest now.

The Darkness comes
to settle your agitated mind
and soothe the ragged edges
of your troubled thoughts.
Weariness and woe
settle to the bottom
of a Deep Pond . . .
and tomorrow, all is born anew.

The mirrors where we see ourselves reflected,
without mercy,
are covered and still.
A new dream is waiting to be birthed.

The Magic of it All

The Thunderbirds are singing.
Their Voices
roar across the sky.
Lightning comes to dance,
to touch the Earth,
brilliant with tendrils of white Fire.

Their song of Power
brings the Rain.
Dripping from the pinions of vast wings,
pitter-pattering upon the leaves,
dripping in free fall from the tops of trees.

The Rain comes to heal the land,
pouring sustenance
down velvet throats of flowers
waiting to be blessed.

Is this Magic?
Is it Love?
Is it Wonder?
It is everything.

The Great Mystery touches All.
Try as we might,
we can not understand it.

We sit in awe,
marveling,
and open our Hearts
to the Power of Love.

Ayal Hurst

RELATIONSHIP

Ayal Hurst

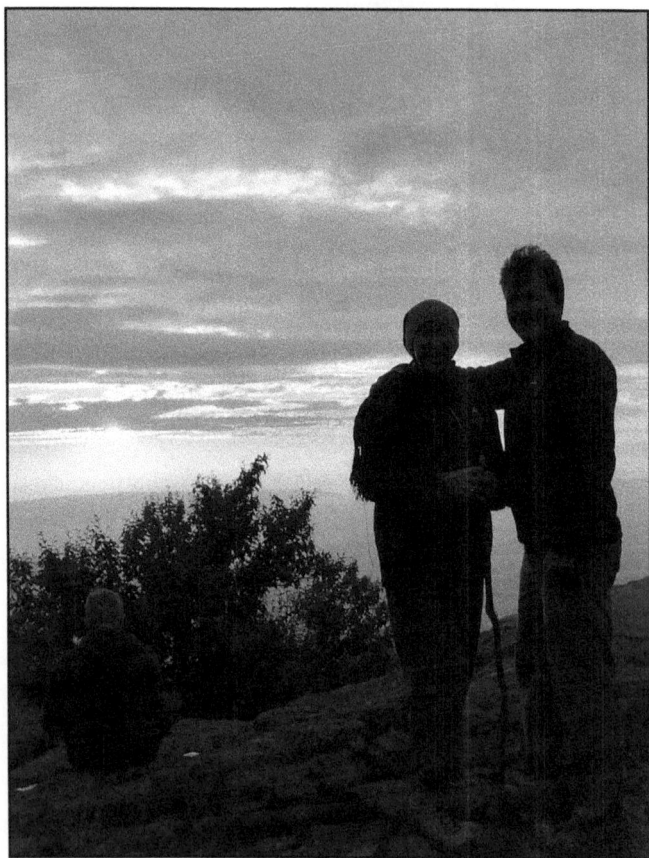

A Love Song

We are older now,
our smiles, not so white,
our bodies spreading out
like sturdy trees,
leaves torn and tossed
by years of storm and wind.

We have shared grief and loss,
glee and rage, joy and death.
We have shared friends,
and flaws, and fears.

Making our way,
bushwhacking
through unmarked trails,
led astray by ego,
false beliefs and arrogance.
Eventually,
we find our way
to healing.

Groping for the Light within.
Missing it,
finding it again.
Like a fine, potential wine
growing clearer
as it ages,
diluting impurities.
Silt drifting to the bottom of our souls,
to float away.

Ayal Hurst

The Fragile Self

Who does not have a fragile self?

The Solitary Dancer
must never surrender blindly
to the blazing roar of the world,
or let oneself be dazzled . . .
or subdued,
by those with Breaths of Fire,
piercing thought and skin.

Hold on to Stillness.
Know the Heart
of your wondrous, rhythmic Soul.
Your journey has the warm, bright Magic
through which every cell is healed.

Listen . . .
Eternity calls your Name.

The Perils of Symbiosis

The Universe delights in combining cells.
Single organisms slip and slide into each other,
joining . . . a new being birthed.

A vast multitude of forms
spring from the passion to unite.
To merge, to create,
to remind the world that All Is One.
Myriads of unending shapes evolve,
dependent upon each other to survive.

As human beings, there is a threat
in deep dependence.
We thrive as separate cells,
singly, not united.

If we refuse this structure, attempt to coil our energy,
as vines will strangle living trees,
in a desperate need to cling,
this violates natural law. A dark abyss is birthed.
There is a peril in symbiosis.

Are we meant to live as conjoined twins,
one entity, at odds within its fractured self,
crippled, inseparable,
cobbled in a strange configuration?
Two heads, sharing arms, legs, spinal cords,
organs, and toes, an ungainly mishmash
of horrific parts?

⇨

Something has gone awry in this unnatural joining.
Separate beings must find their way, unencumbered,
to determine their existence.

Each must walk an untouched path,
chosen with free will.
This is a birthright given to us all.
Two people must have separate forms.
Boundaries and membranes must remain intact.

Too immeshed, entangled in another,
the Way is lost. It has gone too far.
The joining is too deep.
Addicted to each other, nervous systems intertwine
and cannot be unwound.
Such conjoined systems cannot function on their own.
Freedom is impossible, tangled in a web of such
distorted need.

This is a misunderstanding of the tenants of
Relationship, the right to individuate,
to create one's own domain, to make a choice,
to have ownership of Oneself.
Salvation is a distant dream.
The shadow of death looms which each attempt
made to separate this conjoining.

Solitary in nature, whole unto oneself,
each person has been given all they need
to self-generate, self-determine.
By honoring this, you love another best.

Decisions, consequences,
inspiration, finding allies,
finding answers, conquering demons . . .
this is the Hero's Journey.
We gather strength and wisdom
traveling our own road.

The Art of Living

On my kitchen table
a stone of pyrite glints,
nestled in a clay bowl
etched with leaves;
the Tao Te Ching - a small book,
bringing to my hands
the wisdom of the ages;
dahlias and sunflowers,
translucent in the sun;
an embroidered cloth,
sparkling with glitter and beads.

"What do you do with your life?"
my father used to ask me,
as I stood frozen,
a statue made of stone,
a hunted deer.

Had I been capable, older, wiser,
standing in Power,
further back in Time,
I would have smiled softly
and said to him:
"I practice the Art of Living,
O father mine."

Your eyes, though,
will never see me.
This is something that I know.

I speak to the rocks, the trees,
the black crows flying past.
I create beauty, in art, in words.
I strive for balance,
freed from old agenda.

I live with Mystery,
in Stillness,
owned by no one.
I ponder deeper thoughts,
wondering at the workings
of a vast Universe.

I pause,
and choose to speak
from Love.
I have learned
not to harm another.
Kindness, the choice of my religion.

Whether or not
you can understand,
I have healed the family lineage
from generations past,
as I myself transform.
I walk between the worlds,
on etheric planes,
in ways you cannot fathom.

"What do I do with my Life?"
I have learned that
I am enough.

Dancing in the Kitchen

At night,
dancing in the kitchen,
spontaneously we come together,
moved by the music's rhythmic beat
as dinner simmers on the stove.
We whirl, twirling, laughing,
bumping hips, connecting,
freeing ourselves
in gyrations of delight.

Afterwards, I catch my breath,
still enthralled with what we have . . .
with what we have allowed ourselves to be.

Yet, I begin to wonder . . .
what would our
grown children think?
Would they roll their eyes?
Would they turn away?
Will they ever see us, know us,
accept us, for who we truly are?

Could they ever share
in what we love,
dance with us,
when music lures us to be wild and free?
Revel in the Magic,
treasure the forest and the rushing streams?
A sense of loss descends,
a sorrow for the could have beens.
What if wishes sear my soul.

Could I have done it differently?
The music fades, and spirals into loneliness.

The I Ching would counsel me, and say:
Do not be swept up in desire.
Do not desire to change a relationship,
or to impact one.
Do not lose your composure . . . or yourself.
If paths meet, fine. If not, fine.

Stay steady on your Path.
Be Mindful, step by step.
Gain your Inner Independence
and journey to Enlightenment.
Follow in the footsteps of the Sage,
detached and free.

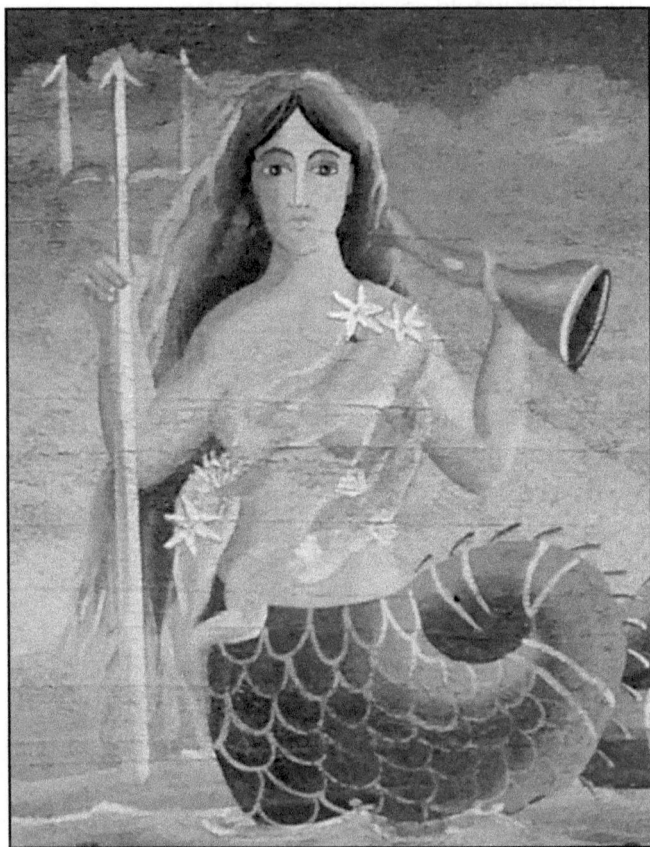

We Are Fire and Water

There were so many years
when I did not understand.
When I felt lost, and bereaved.
I wanted you to touch me,
as Water bends a reed
and trickles over stone.

I wanted you to flow with me,
singing watery songs,
caressing me with silken fingers
that slid and slipped across my skin,
the barest whisper of a touch,
 nearly invisible,
as water carries sound.
I thirsted
for waves of silent knowing,
shared in silken moments,
that could flow between us.

But . . . you cannot be Water.
That is what I am.
My water surges over stones
to weave my way into the world.
Waves flow, fluid and free,
cresting the debris of fractured, shattered dams
to find a form that holds my soul.
I am streaming shades of twilight,
not bound to any form.
You cannot hold it. It Merges with the One.

⇨

I flow unto Myself,
reveling in that cool and liquid flow.
A balm of sound and song fill my worn places,
soothing the unknown path ahead,
the vast and epic journey to the Sea.

You are FIRE.
You burn fierce, so hot and high.
You spin with flame,
a ceaseless, molten energy.
You are a Force of Nature,
Elemental. A hawk who seeks its prey.
Power radiates. Moods shifting,
fiery forms building, rising,
collapsing, once again.
So intense, at times, a scorching heat,
it leaves me parched,
beached alone upon hot sands.

The fury of the world
implodes within your veins.
You seek to burn away the dross
to make things right.
A depth of longing rages deep within
to purify the old and birth the world anew.

When this explosion flares,
a consuming lava of despair,
my Water will flow in.
"Relax . . ." the water whispers.
"The flow will take us where we need to go. . . .

Trust . . . trust . . . be soothed . . . let go of rigid forms . . .
Surrender . . . all is well. There is no consuming need."
Aggression wavers and is still.

I no longer need you to be Water,
You do not have to be different.
I sit by the Fire
and watch your flames
reflect within my eyes,
Warming, sheltering me,
singing a Song of Power,
shooting sparks into the sky.

It is not my power.
But . . . it is a power
that I can take into my heart
and feel the marvel of its Light.
I flow around it, revel in it,
and let it be.

Friends

There are a few, rare friends
who love me as the Poet,
who find sweet words,
filled with wisdom and delight,
to start my day.
They are weavers, dancers, healers . . .
Wise women all.

They are esoteric, unique,
grown deep by Life.
The ones with Sacred names,
playing ukuleles,
and singing to the dawn.

They know who I am.
I speak to the trees,
to an owl, or a crow.
I sit in silence,
staring at the sky.
They understand, and know
I am not mad.

They share my poetry,
walking in the depths with me,
applauding when one births.
Together, we sit, a Circle of Women,
honoring the Moon.
For this, I cherish them.

I have gathered Knowledge
through lifetimes, untold incarnations.
They eagerly receive it,
the deep visions
flowing through my mind,
the wisdom flowing from my lips.

It is not "me".
It is the Cosmos
running through my veins.
They accept that,
and delight
when Spirit reaches through me
to touch those
who want to learn
to heal themselves.

These women fill my path
with companionship and comfort,
for I am one who lives,
solitary,
at the edge of the village,
as shamans did, of old.

They are a wealth of riches
as I thread my way
through sunlight and dark shade.
Their bright essence
shines within my eyes.

⇨

They yearn for Evolution,
making epic journeys
of their own,
through Darkness, through peril,
to reach the endless Light.

They see Beauty in my Path,
and honor it,
when others shook their heads,
and scoffed,
seeing only folly.

Giving

Is it possible to give too much?
Absolutely . . .
when there is a haunted, desperate Need to give,
a trembling fear to be alone.
Helpless, sensing all is chaos, beyond control,
no resonance to receive.

A threat looms deep within.
It births this overflow, this need to Give.
A Dark Shadow whispers:
"Life is dangerous, indeed!"
Believing it, Giving morphs,
becoming strict control.
Danger must be ruthlessly expunged.
All gates, where energy might flow in,
must be firmly bolted shut.

Holding a strict vigil,
a needed service rendered,
a stalwart sentinel poised
against unforeseen consequence,
the Giver then demands appreciation.
A demand for gratitude that cannot come,
for the walls of this Giving
are unreceptive.
They have concretized, impenetrable.

This giving has a cost.
A prison for those who must receive it.
Bound tight within this web,
a deep indebtedness has been instilled.

⇨

The fierceness of this need,
to protect, to be a shield against
the dark of Night, the terrors of the Deep,
creates a ragged prey.
It must lessen another
to ease the fear
of opening, and of loneliness.
The Giver claims the final word,
the only voice.
The other weakens,
boneless,
with no foundation of their own.

A barren, grey domain ensues.
Trust has withered into crumbled shale.
There is no pleasure in this giving.
No safety
It is a hungry sieve, never to be filled.

In such a state,
the Cosmic axis tilts.
The Sacred Seat,
the 2nd Chakra Wheel grows dim.
It cannot offer its fundamental law,
that pleasure is to be both
given and received.
Stunted and still,
the Balance has been lost.

Eventually, the Giver must devolve.
The cost of giving in this way
cannot be sustained.
Their body pays the cost.
Alone and isolated, fearing danger,
seeking ultimate control,
no nourishment is received. Life force cannot flow.
The back has no support.
Hips freeze. Muscles spasm, pain flares.
Forward motion stalls.
The Essence of Yin and Yang disturbed.

Ayal Hurst

For You

After 30 years,
we don't talk constantly,
as I once thought we should,
bantering, filling up the empty spaces
when there is nothing more to say.

Dreamy, starlit eyes
do not gaze coyly at the other.
It is not the hot love you see
plastered on a movie screen.
We do not resemble couples
with well oiled, perfect bodies
leaping in the surf,
white smiles gleaming.

We are something other . . .
something beyond these words,
something that this poem, I know,
will struggle to express.

Our days are spent,
in our own way,
connecting through the hours,
here and there,
a look, a hug, a kiss,
a moment.
We listen to the other
recount their day, their observations,
triumphs, their tribulations.

How can I share what this is,
this union that we have?
It is an excavation, vast in depth,
a monumental structure,
continuing to unfold
in wisdom and in truth.

Strong and resilient,
even when the fierce winds blow.
I see it rising, a cone of energy,
from Earth to Sky, and back again,
multidimensional, multi-hued.
We build it, and traverse it,
this swirling path,
without a map to guide us.
A foundation built through Time.

MOM

My mother has been dead, now,
for three, long years.
She was tiny and bird wristed.
A Force of Nature.
Brilliant. Confused, Adamant. Unrelenting.
I miss her.

Despite all else, she was mine.
And I was hers.
Nothing could change that,
even when estrangement
was a bitter taste between us.

Now, she's gone, a vacuum left in space,
a space she held, at times,
white hot as an unforgiving flame.
I want to reach into the ether,
grab onto something solid,
call her on some Cosmic phone, and say:
"Mom. I'm sick. Mom! I'm sad.
I am happy, tired, thrilled,
forlorn, lonely, delighted.
Mom . . . Mom . . . Mom . . .
Tell me I am special, loved.
Tell me, no matter what I do, or where I go,
there is one place I can come home to."

For 88 years she was so Tangible.
Sharing life together, I knew that someone in this
huge realm of the Cosmos
always loved me, would wrap me up and listen.
I miss her . . . because she belonged to me.

A True Marriage

We began as frightened children, threatened,
raw, wounded. Intimacy was a trap,
a looming Shadow tangling us in chains.

We find re-birth together,
through the fires of evolution,
rising like the Phoenix,
different, wiser, continually reborn.
Finding our way forward, up rocky paths
and narrow, leaf strewn trails.
Sometimes, we stumble.
Sometimes, we are majestic.
Formidable in our combined strength.

We breathe together in our sleep,
reaching, for a moment,
to touch an arm, a hand, a foot, a leg.

We are woven together, sometimes in pain,
sometimes not, sometimes close, sometimes from afar,
It is not easy, this epic path of life. It is challenging,
glorious, exhausting, immense. We do our best.

Slowly we have opened, slowly grown,
through brambles and devotion.
Laughter and tears fertilize our hearts,
learning to forgive the most egregious of hurts.
No matter what I did . . . my husband loved me still.
I learned to love by watching him love me.

⇨

Ayal Hurst

Diving deep beneath the imperfections
and the flaws, I hold the essence of my husband,
the rich, multi-hued tapestry of his soul, and my own,
in the open chasm of my heart, remembering.

As Rumi knew, there is a field so far beyond
the thorny vale of "right" and "wrong."
We do our best to meet each other there.

We function differently.
We strive to understand how we are made.
I slow him down. He lures me on,
trudging through the murky realms of doubt,
trusting that the transformation needed will arrive.
Paths both separate, divergent,
and yet, in many ways, so very much the same.

Once upon a time, I thought the one I loved
must be perfect . . . had to be everything for me.
I thought that his perfection
would show the world how good I was,
the worth that I had finally attained.
I was lost in the illusion of a fairy tale,
unable to love anything that was not
always beautiful, consistent pure . . .
and so, I did not truly love.

We learned to speak with kindness,
affirming Life, despite the horrors of our past.
We have been softened by the Sands of Time,
learning to tread carefully with each other's
vulnerable and fragile hearts.

What is a true marriage?
It happens when you fall in love,
over and over again, with the same person.
Because you choose to grow.

Alone

The rain
softly drumming on the roof,
the fire chortling in the stove,
a chipmunk
running past the window . . .
they keep me company
when you are gone.

WILD LIFE

A Ferocious, Feline Woman

I savor Life, a ferocious, Feline woman
drinking deep from streams of knowing,
listening to the Raven's Call.

This life is Sacred, one of Dance, and Fire, and Decay,
a vast Breath that changes with the Wind.
I choose my life, using it wisely to roar rivers
of translucent healing.
I live every secret rhythm,
laughing with hot desire to devour Time.

I am not born for a world built of broken steel
and cold, concrete debris.
I am after Sacred Magic,
the music of soft rains that kiss my naked skin,
and the tops of towering Trees.
I let my Heart journey, solitary,
through fevered, black storms
and liquid fire.

The Ancestors of my Being,
Deer, Coyote, Bear, Wolf, and Crow,
remember the Ancient Wisdom
and whisper Wild Truths
that ricochet from the canyon walls
and mountain peaks
to hunt the veils that haunt me,
shredding the curtains of illusion.
What besides this, is dancing with Eternity?

Ayal Hurst

A Silent Song of Snow

A silent song of snow drifts to earth,
filling every nook, every cranny,
softly, steadily, effortlessly
painting the world
in a virgin cloud of white.

A peaceful blanket
covering rooftops, trees, and stones,
creating crystal sculptures
in the frozen stream.

The Wind begins to frolic . . .
mighty gusts sweeping past my window
showing me how powerful it can truly be.
I oblige, gasping in delight.

Riding the cold breath of the Wind,
gleeful flakes whirl upward,
caught within the vortex
of a dancing swirl,
passing their brethren who are more sedate,
and properly descending.

Small birds flit to the feeders
we have stationed here and there.
Back and forth, back and forth,
taking hungry turns
to insure their survival.
So cold beneath their feathered robes . . .
no choice but to stoically bear the storm.

I wonder if they have a place of refuge,
somewhere to go,
or if they can only tuck their tiny heads
beneath their wings,
making no sounds of misery.
Perhaps this mute acceptance
is all they know.
Winter comes, as expected,
part of the natural flow of Life.

This is how we need to be:
a silent song . . .
Sisters of the Snow . . .
knowing that the purity of our intent,
that what is good and true within us
transforms all, filling everything we touch
with the softest covering of kindness.

No forceful movements,
no jagged edges,
a refuge in ourselves.
Only gentleness offered,
our giveaway, compassion,
a gift quietly bestowed to balance
the silent roaring of the storm.

Our Life

We delight when the ravens come,
calling to us from the sky,
messages of Magic tucked
deep within their wings,
black and shining as the Void.
We note the direction of their flight.
It tells us what will come,
and where to go.

Colorful stones and nests of birds adorn our home.
We sit together, hidden on a forest trail
beneath the towering trees,
human mushrooms,
rooted in the wonder of the woods.
I read him poems, he tells me stories.

We revel in the rain,
gazing at the water flowing free,
pouring down the mountain side.
The birth and death of growing things.
An emerging bud,
the texture of bark,
a hillside waving in the wind.

Enchanted, hand in hand,
we listen to the Deep Silence, the nursery of Life,
beneath a sky rich with stars,
watching fireflies dance. Our fingers interlace,
cherishing the mystery of living things.

Days of art,
flute songs wafting in the wind,
seedlings tended,
baskets filled with harvest,
apples plucked from gnarly trees,
honeybees dancing on a flower,
adding sweetness to the world.

Enveloped by the Presence of the Earth.
This is the essence of our lives.

⇨

We are stewards of this land,
offering it as refuge
for those who choose to come.
A Sacred Sanctuary,
for the deer, who eat our roses,
for the groundhog in his den.
For the bear, who leaves footprints in our garden,
seeking food and a cave in which to rest.

In this we are as One,
our Dharma strong and clear.

Little Grey Mouse

A little, grey mouse
caught in the trap.
So small,
so alone in death.

I feel forlorn to see it there, abandoned.
A life of curiosity
and twitching whiskers,
ended.

"There is no safety here!"
I yelled to the survivors,
hiding in the crannies of our house.
"Find your nook in Nature!
You belong there, in safety, under trees and sky.
We are frightening!
Territorial and Unforgiving. Unrelenting!
This house is Death, with fangs of steel!
If you venture here for warmth, for ease,
a cruel fate will await you! Be warned!"
I said, in horrified despair. "You *must* go!"

Perhaps they heard me . . .
I hope they did.
I hope a massive, mouse exodus has occurred,
that they have left,
belongings carried on their backs,
crumbles of stored cheese and bread,
tiny pink babies in their mouths.
Perhaps there are small, cozy caves and holes
waiting for them beneath the trees.

The Hummingbird

A tiny hummingbird flies through the rain
to take refuge, lingering,
for just a moment,
on a feeder filled with nectar.

She perches there,
alert, and drinks deep,
for she is wet and cold.

I sit, still as stone,
afraid to move until she is replete.
If I blink an eye, she will fly away,
her Sanctuary lost.

Light

I remember . . .
a shining drop
of water on my skin.

Crystal dewdrops
nestled in a flower's heart.
This world is made of Light.

A Wild Wind

A wild wind roared
through the forest last night.
A fearsome, torrential sound.
Gleeful in ascendancy and might.
An unstoppable Force.

With a gale of fierce laughter,
the wild hands of the Wind
lifted the wooden glider on our porch,
flinging it into the rock strewn creek,
effortlessly, as a brittle leaf swept away
in a swirling gust of air.

The Wind rattled
the heavy timbers of our house.
Shaking the foundation,
shaking us from sleep.
Shaking our perceived safety,
shaking the fallacy we had,
that our civilized shelter
would protect us
from the force of Nature's might.

With morning,
a sense of uncertainty prevailed,
a sense of subtle helplessness.
We felt fragile, fragmented.
Gripped by an unnamed terror
hiding in the darkest corners
of our minds,
not understanding why.

In the wild breath of the Wind,
we had been forced to remember:
life is ephemeral, fleeting,
impermanent.

Old fears are triggered
in the aftermath
of such unquenchable
and primal force.
We struggle, unconsciously,
to reassert Power,
some dynamic of control.

We journey into high alert,
ready to fight or flee,
fearing unseen enemies.
Our bones quiver.
The Center can be lost.

Yet, with this terror comes
surprising jubilation . . .
We feel exhilarated,
freed from the captivity
of illusion, of ownership.

Standing, still whole, surviving
the ferocious heart
of the storm.
Freed from striving,
from holding on
to that which can never
be held.

⇨

The wise sages advise us,
during times of fright and fear,
during times of exultation,
let your heart be pure.
Watch the turmoil of the world,
and let it be.

Return to serenity, they say.
Immerse yourself in the awe
and wonder of the Tao,
which holds infinite galaxies
in the nucleus of an atom.

In that way,
we are ready
for whatever life may bring,
including Death.

Rooting

I have rooted in this land,
this magical, green kingdom of ours,
where the world does not intrude.
I have become part of the grass,
the rocks, the forests, and the sky.
Each day, a flower births.

Encircling the boundaries of our domain,
the stream is a lightness of being
flowing past our feet.

⇨

Ayal Hurst

Twilight comes.
We stand in the doorway facing West.
A gift of sunset flares, the Omega of the day.
At times, a mist of grey and fog
will creep down from the mountain tops,
hiding the horizon,
as we are hidden in its mystery.

We are no longer troubled
with the fear and fury that exists
beyond the boundaries of our home.
It moves with voracious speed and rage.
We have become slow and steady,
quietly growing.
Enamored with the beauty
of the smallest bud and twig.

We wait for robins to arrive in early Spring,
offering a welcome glimpse of color
to a landscape still brown and dun at Winter's edge.

They come when the first, golden blooms
adorn the Forsythia bushes
standing sentinel before our garden gate.

We listen to the croaking chant
of wood frogs as they mate to lay their eggs,
a melody of rich fertility and hope.
We look for bear tracks in the mud,
shivering in primal bliss
when the howls of coyotes echo in the night.

Here and there, I lay a fallen branch
upon a naked hill, eroded by time,
wounded by the works of man.
Roots of trees exposed.
It has a chance to heal,
to catch the leaves that drift to earth in Fall.

We sing to the koi.
Flashing metallic colors from their watery domain.
They maneuver close to shore,
hoping for food when our footsteps resound,
stirring the depths of their elemental home.

The trees allow their roots
to intertwine with the Mother's love.
We see them, branches raised in prayer,
giving homage to the Sky.
Like the trees, our roots are deep,
our arms reach high to celebrate.
We are nourished, balanced,
living in the Center,
children of both Heaven and of Earth.

Medicine Wheel

The Medicine Wheel lies in a quiet glade
behind the old tobacco barn.
Four pure, white stones, larger then the rest,
equidistant from each other, catch the eye.

These are the guardians of The Directions,
North, South, East, and West,
portals we must enter, leading to unopened doors.
Gifts of crystals grace the ground before them.

The Wheel waits quietly for pilgrims seeking answers,
supplicants who yearn for solace,
to rest, embraced in the soft spell of the Sacred,
protected, for a moment,
from the turmoil of the world.
It is hallowed ground.
Enlightenment can be found there,
whispered wisdom drifting in the shaded air.

On days when I am lost,
I seek The Wheel to soothe my soul.
It calls to me, a presence laced
with silent Potency, the deep love of belonging.

Hands in Namaste, I stand,
head bowed, reverent,
just outside the circle, beside the Eastern stone,
the place of Springtime and the rising dawn.

May I enter?
A caress upon my heart,
an invitation offered,
a Mother's arms opening to receive me.

Silently, I step within.
The Circle of Life surrounds me.
A hologram of Being,
the Universe unfolds,
a cornucopia rising to the Sky,
to unknown realms,
on and on, into Infinity.
Each winding whorl,
a lifetime lived
as we traverse The Wheel.

Guidance beckons.
I am called to sit
beside the Southern Stone,
The Golden Gateway.
Here, Coyote rules.
He guards this flaming door.
It leads to innocence returned,
Love remembered.
A soothing balm to childhood wounds.

I have come there to remember.
There is magic in the soft wings of a butterfly.
I am a child again,
in the hot sunshine of Summer meadows,
romping in both shadow and the light.
The memory of forgotten days.

⇨

Beneath my hand, the stone pulses, warming
as my fingers stroke its textured landscape.
I know Coyote watches me, amused,
as I stumble, lost in misconceptions,
lost in the seriousness of my life.

He is there, The Trickster,
knowing I am easily mended, so easily healed.
I only I need to know the steps of the Wild Dance.
Leaping high, he lands beside me,
a playful, roaring wind, a mad howl of delight.

"Why are you here?" he inquires.
Pearly fangs, so close, so sharp,
drip rainbow strands that flow into the Earth
and soon emerge as butterflies.
"I don't know", I reply.
"Are you Dancing?" he asks of me, snuffling at my face.
"No", I say.
"How well do you love?" he asks.
"Not well, yet," I answer, with a weary sigh.
"Ah. Sit for a while with me," he says,
eyes large as the liquid moon.

And so, we sit there, Coyote and me,
as grains of Awareness slowly trickle in.
Above us, the sky, a vast, blue vault.
Swaying to the rhythm of the clouds,
the tall trees Dance.

Ayal Hurst

EVOLUTION

The Cauldron

Shadows begin to swirl,
rising up . . . ancient wraiths of mist and angst
shivering to be released.
The most tenacious darkness can be redeemed,
recapitulated in the Cosmic Cauldron,
reborn, transmogrified,
a new essence purified to begin anew, waking.
If we recognize them.
Allow ourselves to claim them.

The Goddess stirs the Cauldron,
holding a long stave of golden light.
Her brow is made of stars.
She is standing vigil, a sentinel of Grace.
The Dispeller of Illusions,
her staff will sweep away what has been disowned,
what troubles we will sacrifice
in order to be free.

The healing waters of the Cosmos wait.
She asks us to submerge,
to swim in the Cauldron
with our demons,
until they melt away.
"Step in", the Goddess says,
and leads you down cool marble steps
to bathe
in the Violet Waters of Transmutation.
"Do not think", she says
"Rest. Let go. I will take it."

Once upon a Time

Once upon a time,
I was a woman made of glass,
splintering with every word uttered
and every word heard.

My world was shaped from shadows,
ancient patterns, hard and brutal whispers.
Insidious, telling me
I was not good enough,
wise enough, smart enough,
beautiful enough . . . inadequate.
Knowing nothing else, I believed them.

My world was grief filled,
a collapse,
A frantic defense.
I found myself exhausted,
lacking, in some fundamental way.
My shoulders bowed, heavy laden
with chips of broken glass.

Bludgeoned, bruised, without a voice,
my swollen heart would wail,
"How dare you treat me this way?"
A tiny victim, lost in a world of power
beyond my reach.

Now, I am made of rich, tree bark
and deep, strong roots.
I speak to the Wind, and it answers me,
whispering of exotic realms.
And I stand, firmly rooted
in the wildness of my Being.

I see others lost in a morass of glass,
thinking they must fight or fly away.
Thinking they must control, or be controlled,
waiting for their spirit to break
upon an unsafe shore.
Waiting for a monster's boot to come
and force them to the earth.
They falter through their life,
jagged shards upon the ground,
their voices tentative and small.

I know this place so well. I no longer live there.
I know this place of fragile fragmentation,
I no longer condone it.
I do not welcome it in friends,
or collude with them these days,
attempting to coddle or protect them,
watching them fold and break.

"Stand up!" I shout!
"Speak blinding words of Truth!
There is nothing stronger then what you are.
You are not made of splintered glass,
besieged with cracks and fractures."

They cannot hear me,
though they see me
marching through the ripened fields . . .
massive roots
anchoring every step I take.

Tsunami: **Doing the Work**

I am scraping the ego from my bones,
bloody knot by bloody knot.
A tsunami of pain
is released with every scrape.
It floods my cells.
Perceived patterns of abuse,
betrayal, abandonment, criticism, judgements,
every grisly trauma, every sense of worthlessness
left sticking to the marrow.

My knife has been honed,
sharpened with longing for healing and release,
I will find my way through it,
as a tree will find a way to grow,
despite the barbed wire
biting deep into its bark.

A residue of buried panic beckons me,
rising and falling like the tide, as I walk this road.
At times, I sway precariously,
treading a flimsy bridge
of shredding rope, a faith that flees before me.

If I falter, I will fall into the flames
and lose my way.
Beneath the bridge I cross,
a black chasm looms.
It is the past — a place I will not go.
Carefully, step by step,
I must follow in the footsteps of the Sage.

⇨

With every crossing,
I grope for light
and grasp it in a tight, white fist.
Demons of longing and blindness mock me,
fear that has obscured my sight.
Well-worn passageways have been carved
into my flesh,
neurological pathways frozen in my brain.

False trails lure me.
Blaming others for my pain.
Each step demands
I claim the misconceptions.
Each step, I challenge and expose them.

There is no knowing
how long the crossing takes,
what it will ask of me.
This is my part to do.
When I come to the end of it,
Spirit will reach out to take my hand, offering
salvation and release.

The burdens I carry are my own creations,
lost in the layers of time.
I uproot them.
Once uprooted,
seen for what they are,
they drift away,
dreams that leave when one Awakens.
It is illusion. It is nothing.
Though it seemed so fierce, so true.

A Tsunami of Forgiveness comes,
the antidote that enables me to breathe,
embracing every moment
of a life I had lived
fermenting with false beliefs.

These burning chasms,
infernos of untruths,
so damningly familiar,
remain while we slumber,
confused and lost in our illusions.

I must continue on,
to cleanse my well with Consciousness,
with the Foundation Stones
of all that is Eternal,
the Music of the Spheres.

Doing this,
I drink the crystal Water
of Infinity.

The Path

A moment comes when we must choose
to leap from the mountain top
we worked so hard to reach.

What awaits?
The yawning maw of The Abyss.
Unknown.

A choice arrives . . . a perilous moment,
leaving the life we have, perhaps, cherished,
built stone by stone, inhabited by those we love.
If we leap, we leap for that which is unseen.
A still and quiet darkness
below us, above us, around us
waits for us to choose.
Life and death intertwined within.

The looming Choice of Change . . .
To be something . . . other.
To accept the Leap, or to decline?
Could it be ecstatic?
We do not know.
Can we embrace what we know,
one final time,
and let it die?

Shift our shape, allowing it to swirl into the Universe
to become a different form, to move through life
in a different way,
to travel a far reaching, higher path where, perhaps,
those whom we have loved cannot follow?

Do we go on as before, clutching tightly
to the safety of the world we think we know?
Is it stagnation, comfort?
Do we jump?
Once the leap is made,
there is no point of return.
There is no going back.
There is no point of reference.

We only know
what we know we must have,
what we MUST evolve into . . .
something that is True,
though we may not know its shape.

To enter those Gates of Change,
we cannot nurse our false beliefs
or tow them with us in disguise.
The domain we fly toward lives only,
eternally, in Freedom.

Ayal Hurst

These Days

The hot breath of the house,
rising from the fireplace,
drifts toward an opaque sky,
grey and pearlescent, pregnant with rain,
swirling with the exhaled gusts
of the Wind Messengers.

I find myself, these days,
in a still, sacred bubble,
growing slowly with the forest.
The deep silence of the land surrounds me.

There is no gravitational pull for friends to come,
carrying their unresolved burdens upon their backs.
I feel them struggling, lost under the weight
of their creations, confused.
I no longer try to lift illusions from their shoulders.
If they choose to keep them, I let it be.
The smoky contours of their troubled concepts, a
reality I no longer share, drift away from me.

The clarity of the sacred bubble
I am encased within
remains intact. Translucent.
I see the world differently then they do.
Cause and effect all lie within.

The thoughts within
create the world without.
Reality is a dream.
How clearly we dream
it is entirely up to us.

The personal persona,
its neon colors flashing,
its textures and tangled knots
seems to have flown from me.

More and more, each day.
I am changing.
I no longer participate, sleepwalking,
lumbering through the world
of envy and dense desires,
through dimensions of right and wrong,
blame and shame,
lost in the loneliness
of unconscious dreaming.

Things are becoming lucid.
I have worked diligently to get here.
The Water of my Being is,
finally, winding its way
to previously unchartered realms
where I am as light,
and free,
as a breath of ocean air.

An Unformed Truth

An Unformed Truth births when longed for,
arising from depths previously unreachable,
a dive that, before, was too dangerous to attempt.

Initially, it can be hard to find.
It is a jumbled mass without distinction,
an unseen form . . . the phantom of an idea.
We try to catch it,
words tumbling over themselves.

We try to explain it.
A dream, a shadow sought,
it yearns to surge toward sunlit clarity.

The vague concept of . . . something . . .
we sense it living beneath our attention . . .
we feel it, wanting to emerge,
swimming in the primal deep,
demanding to come forth.
A further truth.
We seek an understanding that is
dripping still with protoplasmic beads of
Unconsciousness.

Not yet corporeal, not yet crystalized,
not yet a vision recognized.
An evolutionary step not yet taken.
It is trying to find its way out of the Darkness,
from the infinite soup of possibilities.
It has been germinating . . . a seed not yet
brought into the Light.

We feel it there, an un-manifested presence
waiting to be found.

How to bring it forth? We dance it.
We speak it.
We paint it.
We shake a poem from our bones.
We sacrifice an old belief we know to be untrue.

We allow it to come forth, though its form
may change as it surfaces
from the unknown, darkest places.
It is an unlit gem
hanging from the ceiling of an inner cave,
embedded in the walls of our soul, waiting.

We chisel at it with our fierce desire to be free.
plunging into uncharted realms of Inner space.
The final frontier.
We call to it, coax it,
willing it to be held in our hand.
We turn it this way and that,
attempting to grasp what it might be.

It rearranges us when it emerges.
We are sharpened, shaped into an unexpected form.
A new Universe unfolds beneath our feet,
an idea, a thought, an epiphany,
a clear path, a new pattern
that flows us forward, carrying us into
our next mysterious cycle of becoming.

Ayal Hurst

After Dark Thoughts

After dark thoughts circle through my naked mind
in the ferocious dark of Night, and hold my heart from
beating, devouring the Breath of Life. . . .

I wake to remember warm breezes on my skin,
the slow melting of sculpted ice,
luminous with Light;
the embrace of wild, green forests, fresh with the
scent of rain,
the magic of a child's first word.

My breath returns.
My heartbeat slow and sure.
And dawn hovers over the horizon.

A Solitary Web

I am a Solitary Web,
the music of angels.
Naked as a breath,
blazing with thought
and the sound of
my still voice.
The Fire's magic murmur.

The Eternal Rhythm
of the vast, deep sky.
I circle in stars
and storm,
and sisters,
through the belly of the Ocean,
through a brilliant Universe.

From Peace
to the wild roar
of the lingering Dark.
From marbled rose
to cool, wet stone,
and the soft, translucent surges
of the rain.

My fevered skin
dances Life's ferocious Dance,
imagining . . .
Never, and always,
Myself.

Ayal Hurst

Listen!

Listen! I have awakened!
Remembering I was broken,
cold and haunted,
a frozen stone, dying,
Disempowered in a prison
whose bars I could not see.

A river not explored,
desires never known,
meager and subdued.
A song unsung.

Now, I know.
I was not born to be subservient,
a placater, abdicating my self,
my place, my right to be,
feared for the potent Woman that I am.

I am not second hand, a lesser being,
indebted to Adam, "the evil of Eve".
I am a Woman no longer bound
by the ferocious will of Man,
of fathers, husbands, brothers, priests, and sons.

Ecstatic, open, full, I am The Goddess,
Creator of all life. The Final Authority.

I am Durga, the Warrior Queen
I am Kuan Yin, Mother of Compassion.
I am Yemaya, sensual, fluid,
unending waves of creative thought.

I celebrate myself.
I am not swayed,
I do not run fleeing
from the bellowing voice of men.

Waterfalls cascade,
frothing crystals from my fingertips.
Within me grow all things.
I shift and morph upon my own command.
I dance. I dream.

Words spoken without fear
wing their way into the world,
butterflies and bright bird song.
I speak my truth.

I am made of storms and visions.
I feel life in every full and brilliant breath.

Longing for Love

Do not long to be loved.
Longing, you deny that it exists.
Longing, you are mired
within a web of sticky threads,
caught within an unlit maze,
the greatest of Illusions.

Do you know that you
ARE Love Incarnate?
You have just forgotten.
It has formed every cell, every breath,
every beat of your Heart.
It is there, within you,
flowing through the Spiraling Universe,
glowing in brilliant strands of golden Light.

"See me! See Me!" you cry.
Chasing love with every breath,
making your deeds known,
seeking validation so intensely
you devour space and air.

Thinking you must change the world,
control everything,
create it in your own image
to know that you are real,
you will be lost
in the foggy labyrinth of your mind.

When all bow to you, agree with you,
hear only you, are a mirror of yourself,
will it fulfill your insatiable hunger
to be loved?
Wounded, the form distorts.

You see yourself a paragon of good deeds.
A benevolent dictator,
the Great, kind Father,
wise in his righteousness, his helpfulness,
knowing how it ought to be,
using your will to overpower,
keeping all things safe, efficient.
Your truth, everyone else's standard.

Will this soothe the burn
and bring you the misplaced balm
of Love you seek?
Other's thoughts, their choices,
a crime in your Kingdom,
a threat to your regime, a rejection of yourself.

Stepping beyond the Stream of Life, into your fear,
tasting it's sour flavor, again and again,
Love flies away from you, illusive.
The current carries you farther and farther away,
your kingdom, an imprisoned swamp
of tangled mangrove roots.

⇨

This is the essence of suffering and damnation.
Spinning and spinning, looping around and around,
blinded by a false belief, following a false trail
as the Universe flows merrily along.

All of Life flows perfectly,
embraced in a Love
beyond the comprehension of your mind.
You do not need to bend the world . . .
only to see it as it truly is.

Love is in all things.
Seeing the God in everything,
knowing yourself to be the love you crave,
your suffering will cease to be.

෴

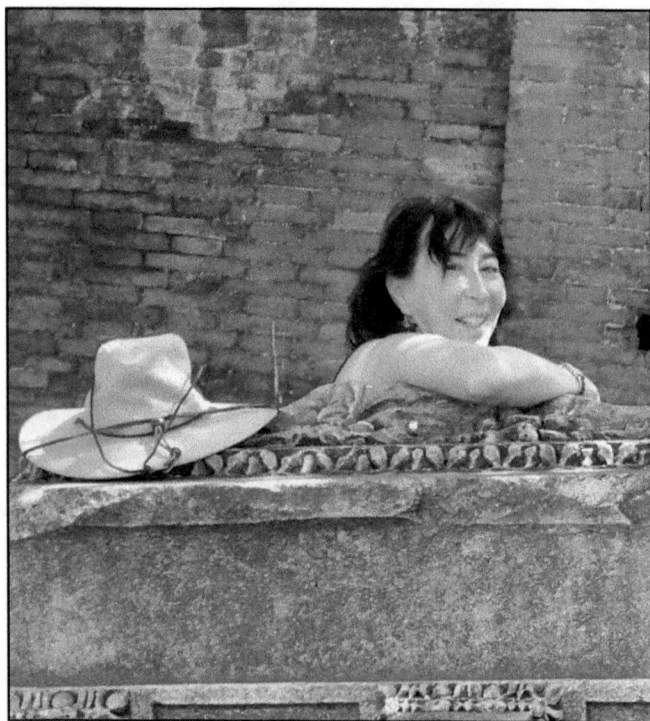

About the Author

Ayal Hurst is an artist, a published author, a Holistic Healer, a Spiritual Counselor, who loves living in the mountains, on magical land, with her husband Hawk. She is honored to be the Mother of Allison and Matt, and the Grandmother of Finn and Liam.

About Pisgah Press & ArsPoetica

Pisgah Press was established in 2011 in Asheville, NC to publish works of quality offering original ideas and insight into the human condition and the world around us. The imprint ArsPoetic was created to help local and regional writers find an outlet for their poetry.

To support the tradition of publishing for the pleasure of the reader and the benefit of the author, please encourage your friends and colleagues to visit www.PisgahPress.com. All Pisgah Press and ArsPoetica releases are available on Amazon.com or on our website. For more information, or to investigate having your own book published, please contact us at pisgahpress@gmail.com.

Also available from Pisgah Press & ArsPoetica

POETRY COLLECTIONS

Talking with Ghosts	Victoria Bender
Letting Go	Donna Lisle Burton
Way Past Time for Reflecting	Donna Lisle Burton
From Roots . . . to Wings	Donna Lisle Burton
This Virgin Page	Jim Carillon
Centered	Jim Carillon
Journeys	Jim Carillon
And to See Takes Time	Mamie Davis Hilliard
Barricaded Bards: Poems from the Pandemic	The Poets of OLLI
Unsent Postcards	Nelson Sartoris
With These Hands	Nelson Sartoris
On Wings of Words	Nelson Sartoris
Brain Slivers	Nelson Sartoris
Invasive Procedures: Earthquakes, Calamities, & poems from the midst of life	Nan Socolow

FICTION

Gabriel's Songbook — Michael Amos Cody

FINALIST, FEATHERED QUILL BOOK AWARD, FICTION, 2021

A Twilight Reel — Michael Amos Cody

GOLD MEDAL, FEATHERED QUILL BOOK AWARD, SHORT STORIES, 2021

Port City — Eliot Sefrin

Trang Sen: A Novel of Vietnam — Sarah-Ann Smith

MYSTERY
THE BOB & MARCUS MYSTERIES

Shade, Fault Line, Rain Winter — H. N. Hirsch

THE RICK RYDER MYSTERIES

Deadly Dancing, Killer Weed, The Pot Professor, Murder on the Rocks — RF Wilson

The Last of the Swindlers — Peter Loewer

NON-FICTION

Musical Morphine: Transforming Pain One Note at a Time — Robin Russell Gaiser

FINALIST, USA BOOK AWARDS, SELF-HELP

Open for Lunch — Robin Russell Gaiser

Reed's Homophones: A Comprehensive Book of Sound-alike Words — A.D. Reed

Swords in their Hands: George Washington and the Newburgh Conspiracy — Dave Richards

FINALIST, USA BOOK AWARDS, HISTORY

Order online from Amazon or B&N, or from:

Pisgah Press, LLC
PO Box 9663, Asheville, NC 28815
www.pisgahpress.com